FLYING GIANTS OF LONG AGO

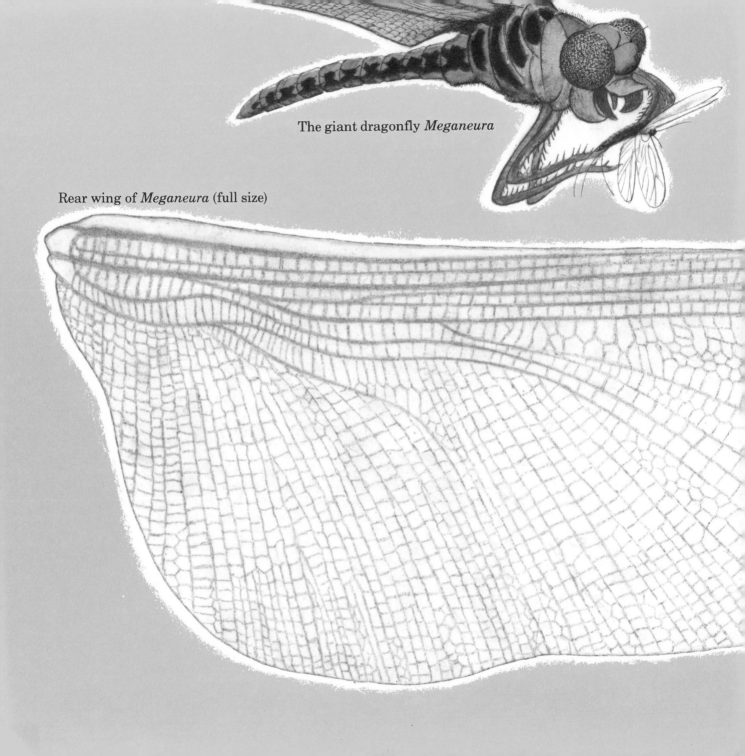

The giant dragonfly *Meganeura*

Rear wing of *Meganeura* (full size)

This Is a Let's-Read-and-Find-Out Science Book®

FLYING GIANTS OF LONG AGO

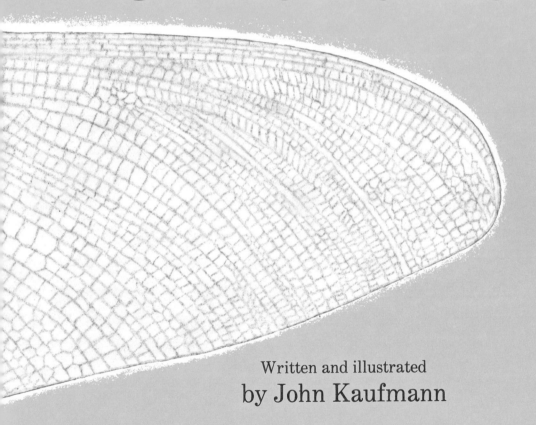

Written and illustrated
by John Kaufmann

Thomas Y. Crowell   New York

Other *Let's-Read-and-Find-Out Science Books*® You Will Enjoy

Bats in the Dark by John Kaufmann · *Birds at Night* by Roma Gans · *Birds Eat and Eat and Eat* by Roma Gans · *Bird Talk* by Roma Gans · *Ducks Don't Get Wet* by Augusta Goldin · *Emperor Penguins* by Kazue Mizumura · *Hummingbirds in the Garden* by Roma Gans · *It's Nesting Time* by Roma Gans · *Little Dinosaurs and Early Birds* by John Kaufmann · *Birds Are Flying* by John Kaufmann

The *Let's-Read-and-Find-Out Science Book* series was originated by Dr. Franklyn M. Branley, Astronomer Emeritus and former Chairman of the American Museum–Hayden Planetarium, and was formerly co-edited by him and Dr. Roma Gans, Professor Emeritus of Childhood Education, Teachers College, Columbia University. For a complete catalog of Let's-Read-and-Find-Out Science Books, write to Thomas Y. Crowell Junior Books, Harper & Row, Publishers, Inc., 10 East 53rd Street, New York, NY 10022.

Let's-Read-and-Find-Out Science Book is a registered trademark of Harper & Row, Publishers, Inc.

Flying Giants of Long Ago
Copyright © 1984 by John Kaufmann
Printed in the U.S.A. All rights reserved.

Library of Congress Cataloging in Publication Data
Kaufmann, John.
   Flying giants of long ago.

   (Let's-read-and-find-out science book)
   Summary: An introduction to prehistoric
insects, birds, and reptiles that flew.
   1. Insects, Fossil—Juvenile literature. 2.
Birds, Fossil—Juvenile Literature. 3.
Pterosauria—Juvenile literature. [1. Pre-
historic animals. 2. Insects, Fossil. 3. Birds,
Fossil. 4. Pterodactyls] I. Title. II. Series.
QE831.K38 1984   560   81-43881
ISBN 0-690-04219-1
ISBN 0-690-04220-5 (lib. bdg.)

3 4 5 6 7 8 9 10

To Franz

Have you ever seen a dragonfly? If you have, you know how big these insects are. Some have wings that measure more than seven inches from tip to tip. But once, there were even bigger dragonflies. They lived millions and millions of years ago, when there were flying insects of many kinds.

Two hundred twenty million years ago, insects were the only animals on earth that could fly. There were no birds then, or bats, or any other flying creatures.

Most flying insects were small. They were about the same size as insects are today. But some were huge.

Megatypus ingentissimus is
four inches bigger than the book you are holding

The dragonfly *Megatypus ingentissimus*
(Meg-a-TEEP-us in-gen-TIS-ee-mus) had wings that
were twenty-one inches across. Like all dragonflies,
Megatypus lived by eating other insects. Twisting
and turning, swerving and swooping, it used its legs
to snatch insects out of the air.

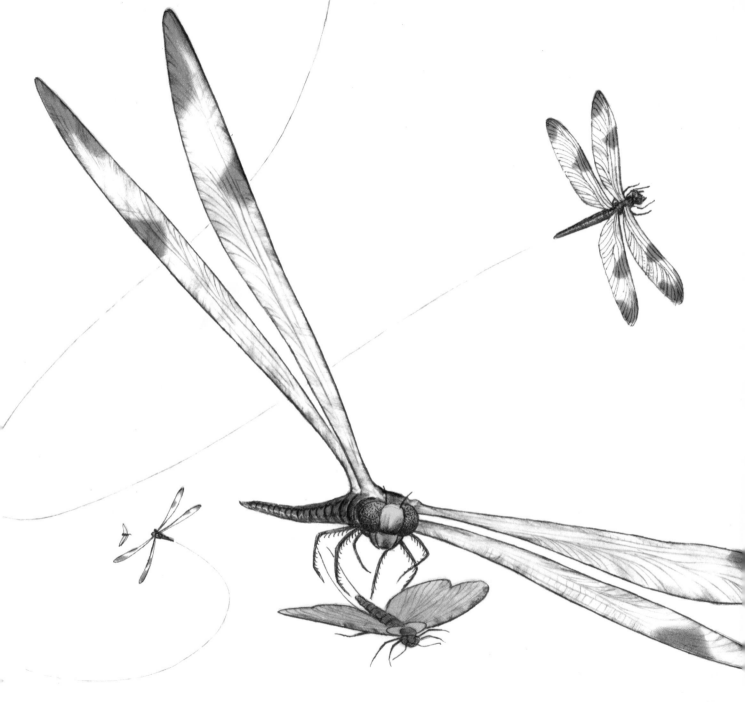

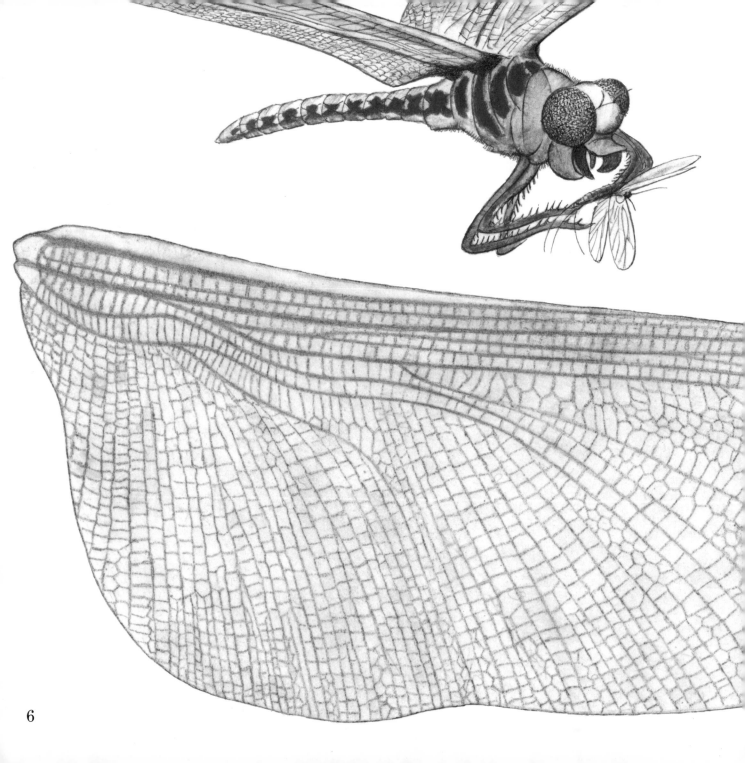

Megatypus was big, but *Meganeura monyi* (Meg-a-NOOR-a MON-yee) was even bigger. Its wings were thirty inches from tip to tip. It had huge bulging eyes, long, spiny legs, and a gaping mouth. It could catch and gobble up almost any other insect. *Meganeura* was king of the air. As far as we know, it is the largest insect that ever lived.

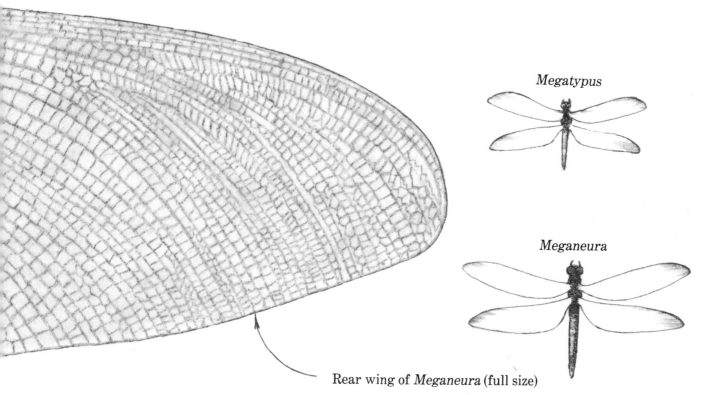

Megatypus

Meganeura

Rear wing of *Meganeura* (full size)

For more than fifty million years, insects had the sky all to themselves. Then other creatures took to the air.

Birds were among the new fliers, and some of them were very big. One was a seabird called *Osteodontornis* (Os-tee-o-don-TOR-nis). It had a wingspread of sixteen feet.

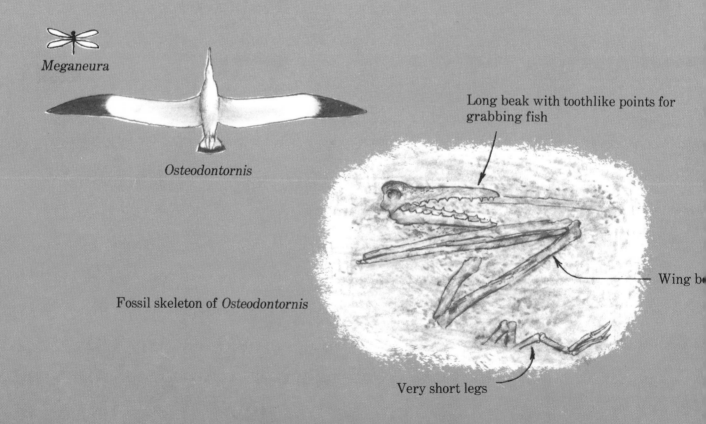

Meganeura

Osteodontornis

Long beak with toothlike points for grabbing fish

Fossil skeleton of *Osteodontornis*

Wing b

Very short legs

Osteodontornis had very short legs,
so it was a clumsy walker.
But it seldom walked.
It lived on the sea. Its short
legs and webbed feet were
fine for swimming.

Giant barn owl

Barn owl of tod:

On land there were giant barn owls called *Tyto* (TIDE-O) owls, whose wings spread six feet from tip to tip. They were one and one half times bigger than barn owls are today. *Tyto* owls hunted at night for ratlike animals called huitas.

Fossil skeleton of a teratorn

Teratorns had feathers on the ends of their wings that spread out like huge fingers.

The sharp beak had a hooked tip for tearing food.

12

The largest birds of all were the teratorns. They were scavengers. They fed on dead animals.

One teratorn had wings that spread seventeen feet across. Scientists called it *Teratornis incredibilis* (Ter-a-TOR-nis in-cre-DEE-bi-lis), the incredible teratorn. They were pretty sure it was the biggest bird that had ever flown.

Teratornis incredibilis

Twenty-five feet!

Teratornis incredibilis

Argentavis magnificens

Magnificent!

Meganeura

But in 1979 in South America a new fossil teratorn was found. It had a wingspread of twenty-five feet. From beak to tail, it was eleven feet long. Scientists named it *Argentavis magnificens* (Are-jen-TA-vis mag-NIF-i-cens), the magnificent bird of Argentina.

When it stood on the ground, *Argentavis* could have looked a tall person in the eye.

Very likely, *Argentavis* is the largest bird that has ever flown. But it is not the largest flying creature of all. That giant of giants is a pterosaur, a flying reptile.

Pterosaurs did not have feathered wings like birds. Their wings were covered with thin, stretchy skin, as bat wings are today. Pterosaurs came in many shapes and sizes.

Dimorphodon

Rhamphorhynchus

Pterodactylus

Pterodactylus

    Some pterosaurs were small, no bigger than a sparrow. Some had small bodies but large wings. *Nyctosaurus* (Nick-toe-SAU-rus) had eagle-sized wings that measured seven feet across. But its body was no bigger than a pigeon's.

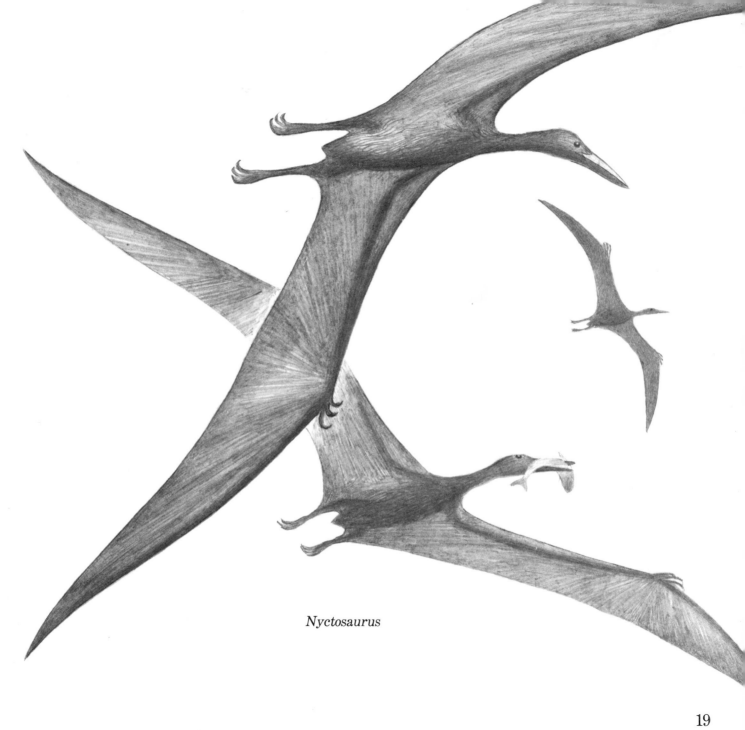

Nyctosaurus

Other pterosaurs were huge. The wings of *Pteranodon* (Ter-AN-o-don) spread twenty-five feet, the same as *Argentavis's*. But its body was smaller and its bones were lighter, so *Pteranodon* weighed much less. It could glide with ease above the waves. It probably flew low, snapping up fish with its pointed beak.

No one really knows why some *Pteranodons* had a large head crest, while others had none.

Pteranodons carried their catch in a throat pouch, the way pelicans do today.

For a long time everyone thought *Pteranodon* was the largest flying reptile of all. But in 1971 in Texas scientists found fossils of an even bigger one. They named it *Quetzalcoatlus* (Ket-sal-KWAT-l-us). Its wings spread forty feet from tip to tip. Scientists believe it is the largest creature that ever flew.

Quetzalcoatlus was bigger than some airplanes.

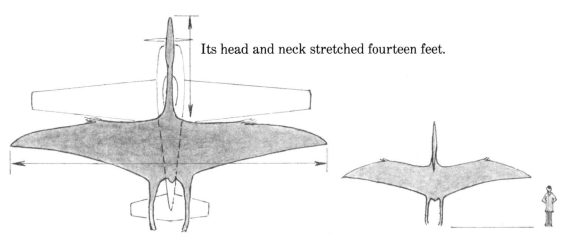

Its head and neck stretched fourteen feet.

Its wingspread reached forty feet.

Pteranodon   Person

Its wings were so huge, *Quetzalcoatlus* probably never flapped them. To take off, it may have jumped from high places and then glided through the air.

Quetzalcoatlus was a scavenger, the greatest of them all. Its long, narrow neck and head could reach deep inside the bodies of dead dinosaurs.

Will bigger flying giants be discovered someday? Probably not. Scientists think *Meganeura*, *Argentavis*, and *Quetzalcoatlus* were as large as creatures of their kind can ever be. But no one can really be certain. Somewhere the fossils of even bigger flying giants may still lie buried in the earth.

Bigger than *Quetzalcoatlus*? Nonsense! No creature that big could have ever flown.

Anyway, I think we should try digging around here.

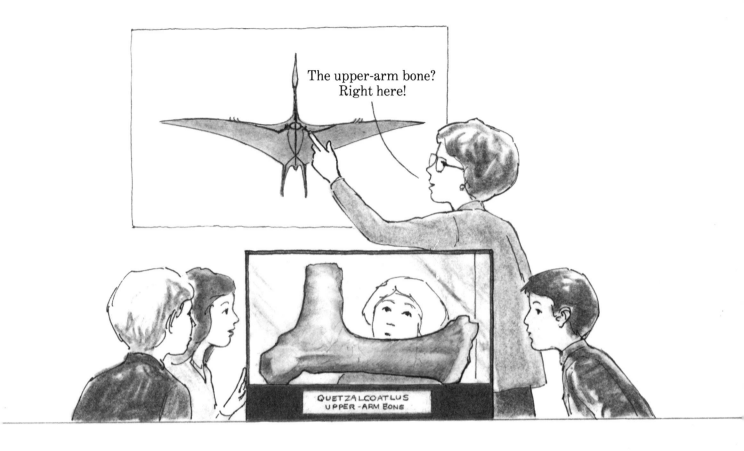

Today there are no pterosaurs, big or small. There are no giant teratorns or giant dragonflies. All these animals are extinct. They vanished from the earth long ago.

Today the biggest dragonfly in the world lives in
South America. It has a wingspread of seven and one
half inches. The biggest insect is a moth from India. Its
wings measure ten inches from tip to tip. And the
biggest bat is the Flying Fox, a fruit bat of Java. Its
wings are five feet across.

Megaloprepus, South America

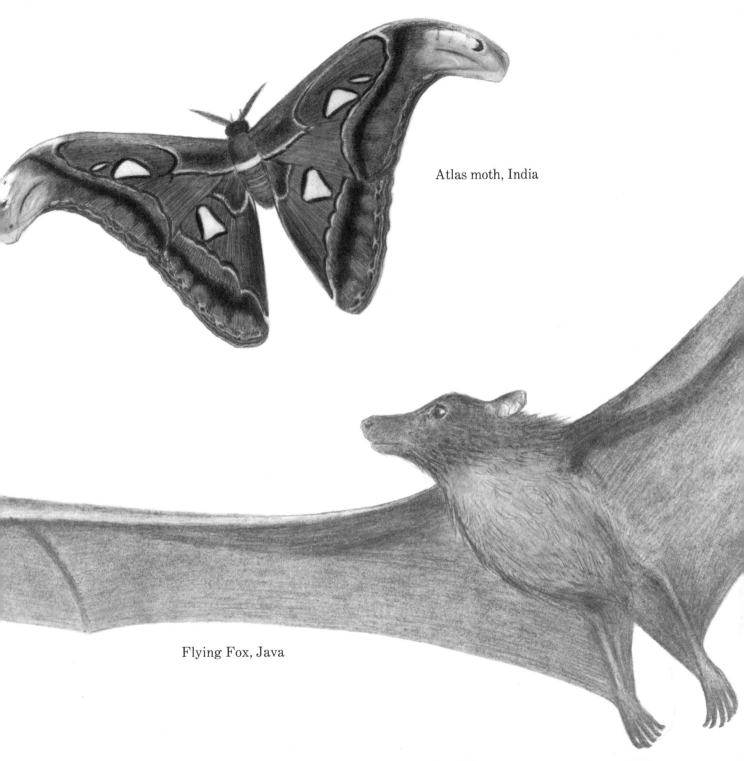

Atlas moth, India

Flying Fox, Java

Today the biggest fliers of all are birds. The South American condor has wings that measure ten feet across.

The wandering albatross glides over the oceans near Antarctica, spreading its huge wings twelve feet.

Someday you may see one of these giants for
yourself. You'll surely see smaller birds and insects
and maybe even bats. When you do, imagine what it
would be like if they were as huge as the flying giants
of long ago.

About the Author

As a child, John Kaufmann says he was fascinated with flight, and he liked to make and fly paper airplanes. Now, years later, his early interest is reflected in the carefully researched, knowledgeable books he writes and illustrates.

A native New Yorker, Mr. Kaufmann was graduated from the Aeronautical Course at Brooklyn Technical High School. He studied art at the Pennsylvania Academy in Philadelphia and during a year's stay in Europe with his wife Alicia. The Kaufmanns and their sons, Darius and Noel, live in Fresh Meadows, New York.